I0774079

IS CAPITALISM SLAVERY?

An Insight Of The Various Systems Of Exploitation And Inequality in the Twenty-First Century

Greg V. Jack

Copyright © 2024

Greg V. Jack

All rights reserved. No part of this publication may be reproduced, distributed, or transmitted in any form or by any means, including photocopying, recording, or other electronic or mechanical methods, without the prior written permission of the publisher, except in the case of brief quotations embodied in critical reviews and certain other noncommercial uses permitted by copyright law.

Table of contents

Introduction

In the annals of history, few questions have stirred as much controversy and debate as the one posed by the title of this book: "Is Capitalism Slavery?" At first glance, the comparison may seem audacious, even provocative. After all, capitalism, with its promises of opportunity, freedom, and prosperity, has long been hailed as the epitome of economic progress and human advancement. Yet, as we delve deeper into the complexities of capitalist systems, we are confronted with uncomfortable truths and inconvenient realities that demand our attention.

The premise of this book is simple yet profound: to critically examine the parallels between capitalism and slavery and to challenge the prevailing narratives that justify and perpetuate systems of exploitation and inequality. For too long, the injustices inherent in capitalist systems have been obscured by rhetoric extolling the virtues of the free market and the invisible hand of the economy. Yet, beneath the veneer of prosperity lies a darker reality: one marked by exploitation, coercion, and the commodification of human lives.

As we embark on this journey of exploration, it is essential to acknowledge the profound impact that capitalism has had on shaping the course of human history. From the rise of industrial capitalism in the 18th and 19th centuries to the neoliberal policies of the late 20th and early 21st centuries, capitalism has left an indelible mark on societies around the world. Yet, as we shall see, this legacy is not one of unbridled progress and prosperity but one of inequality, injustice, and human suffering.

At the heart of the comparison between capitalism and slavery lies the recognition that both systems are rooted in the exploitation of human labor for profit. While the forms of exploitation may differ, the underlying dynamics remain the same: the extraction of surplus value from the labor of others, the concentration of wealth and power in the hands of the few, and the systematic dehumanization of those deemed expendable in pursuit of profit.

Moreover, the parallels between capitalism and slavery extend beyond the economic realm to encompass broader social, political, and cultural dimensions. Just as slavery was justified through ideologies of racial superiority and paternalism, so too is capitalism upheld by ideologies of meritocracy and individualism that serve to justify and perpetuate systems of inequality and injustice.

As we delve deeper into the question posed by the title of this book, it is essential to approach the subject with an open mind and a willingness to confront uncomfortable truths. The goal of this exploration is not to provide definitive answers but to provoke critical reflection and dialogue on the nature of capitalism and its implications for human freedom, dignity, and justice.

In the chapters that follow, we will examine the historical roots of capitalism, explore its fundamental contradictions and injustices, and consider alternative visions of economic organization and social change. Through rigorous analysis, compelling evidence, and thought-provoking arguments, we will challenge the prevailing myths and ideologies that obscure the realities of capitalist exploitation and inequality.

Ultimately, the question posed by the title of this book is not merely academic but one of profound moral and political significance. It is a question that demands our attention and calls us to confront the realities of capitalist oppression and exploitation. It is a question that challenges us to imagine alternative futures and to work towards a world where freedom, dignity, and justice are not just lofty ideals but tangible realities for all.

Chapter 1: Historical perspectives: Following the Development of Exploitative Labor Practices

The argument that capitalism shares similarities with slavery stems from a deep examination of historical perspectives, tracing back to the roots of both systems and their impact on human labor and exploitation. While the comparison may seem provocative at first glance, a closer examination reveals historical connections and parallels that shed light on the complex relationship between capitalism and slavery.

To understand the historical perspective of the argument, it's essential to explore the origins of capitalism and its relationship with labor systems throughout history. Capitalism emerged as an economic system in Europe during the transition from feudalism to industrialization, marked by the rise of market economies, private ownership of property, and wage labor. This period coincided with the expansion of European colonialism and the transatlantic slave trade, which played a significant role in fueling capitalist development.

The transatlantic slave trade, which lasted from the 16th to the 19th centuries, involved the forced migration of millions of Africans to the Americas to work on plantations, mines, and other industries. Slavery provided the labor force necessary for the production of lucrative commodities such as sugar, cotton, tobacco, and coffee, which fueled the growth of capitalist economies in Europe and the Americas. The exploitation of enslaved labor contributed to the accumulation of wealth and capital that underpinned the rise of capitalism.

Moreover, the industrial revolution, which began in the late 18th century, transformed economic production and labor relations, leading to the emergence of wage labor and factory-based production. While capitalism brought about innovations in technology, transportation, and production methods, it also led to the exploitation of workers in factories, mines, and other industries. Working conditions were often harsh, wages were low, and labor rights were limited, leading to widespread discontent and resistance among the working class.

The parallels between slavery and capitalism become apparent when examining the nature of labor relations under both systems. While slavery involved the direct ownership of individuals as property, capitalism relies on wage labor, where workers sell their labor power to capitalists in exchange for wages. While workers in capitalist societies are technically free to choose their employment, they often face economic coercion and exploitation due to unequal bargaining power and systemic inequalities.

Furthermore, the legacy of slavery continues to shape modern capitalist economies, particularly in terms of racial and economic disparities. The exploitation of enslaved labor contributed to the accumulation of wealth and power among white elites, while perpetuating racial hierarchies and inequalities that persist to this day. The exploitation of marginalized and vulnerable populations, including people of color, immigrants, and low-wage workers, reflects ongoing patterns of economic coercion and exploitation within capitalist systems.

The historical perspective on the argument that capitalism shares similarities with slavery reveals deep-seated connections and parallels between the two systems. While capitalism and slavery are distinct forms of labor exploitation, they are rooted in similar dynamics of power, exploitation, and inequality. Understanding the historical context of capitalism and its relationship with slavery is essential for critically examining the impact of economic systems on human freedom, dignity, and social justice.

The Origins of Capitalism in Colonialism and the Transatlantic Slave Trade

The origins of capitalism are deeply intertwined with colonialism and the transatlantic slave trade, two interconnected historical phenomena that played pivotal roles in shaping the economic, social, and political landscape of the modern world. Understanding the relationship between capitalism, colonialism, and slavery is essential for grasping the complexities of economic development and exploitation within the context of global capitalism.

Colonialism refers to the practice of establishing and maintaining colonies in distant territories, often for the purposes of economic exploitation, resource extraction, and political domination. Beginning in the late 15th century with the voyages of exploration and conquest led by European powers such as Spain, Portugal, England, France, and the Netherlands, colonialism led to the establishment of vast empires spanning continents and oceans.

The exploitation of enslaved labor played a crucial role in the accumulation of wealth and capital that underpinned the rise of capitalism in Europe and the Americas. Enslaved people were subjected to dehumanizing conditions, forced labor, and violence, all in the pursuit of profit and economic gain.

Moreover, the transatlantic slave trade and colonialism facilitated the global exchange of goods, people, and ideas, laying the groundwork for the development of capitalist economies and global markets. European colonial powers established trade networks, shipping routes, and commercial hubs that facilitated the flow of commodities such as sugar, cotton, spices, and precious metals between Europe, Africa, the Americas, and Asia.

The origins of capitalism in colonialism and the transatlantic slave trade highlight the interconnected nature of economic exploitation, imperialism, and globalization within the context of global capitalism. Understanding the historical roots of capitalism in colonialism and slavery is essential for critically examining the enduring legacies of exploitation, inequality, and injustice within capitalist societies.

The Industrial Revolution's Impact of Slavery: Human Exploitation and Economic Growth

The Industrial Revolution, which began in the late 18th century in Britain before spreading to other parts of Europe and eventually the world, had a profound impact on the institution of slavery, human exploitation, and economic growth. This period marked a significant shift in economic production, technological innovation, and labor relations, transforming societies and economies in unprecedented ways.

One of the key ways in which the Industrial Revolution impacted slavery was through changes in economic production and labor demand. The rise of mechanized manufacturing, steam power, and new technologies led to increased demand for raw materials such as cotton, sugar, and tobacco, which were produced using enslaved labor in colonies such as the Caribbean and the Americas. The exploitation of enslaved labor became even more crucial to meet the growing demand for commodities in industrializing economies.

Moreover, the Industrial Revolution facilitated the global exchange of goods, capital, and labor, creating new opportunities for the exploitation of enslaved people. The development of steamships, railways, and telegraph lines enabled faster and more efficient transportation of goods and resources between distant regions, facilitating the movement of enslaved people from Africa to the Americas and the Caribbean to meet the labor demands of industrializing economies.

The Industrial Revolution also had a profound impact on the nature of work and labor relations, both in industrialized countries and in colonial territories. In industrialized economies, factory-based production and wage labor became increasingly prevalent, as workers were employed in factories, mines, and other industries under harsh and exploitative conditions. While workers in industrialized economies were technically free wage laborers, they often faced economic coercion, long hours, low wages, and unsafe working conditions, reminiscent of the exploitation experienced by enslaved people.

Furthermore, the Industrial Revolution fueled the growth of capitalist economies and the accumulation of wealth and capital, much of which was derived from the exploitation of enslaved labor in colonies. The profits generated from slave-based industries such as cotton, sugar, and tobacco enriched merchants, landowners, and capitalists, contributing to the expansion of capitalist enterprises and the consolidation of economic power.

However, the Industrial Revolution also contributed to the eventual decline of slavery as an institution, as technological advancements and changing economic conditions made slavery less economically viable. The mechanization of agriculture, the development of alternative sources of labor, and the rise of abolitionist movements all played a role in undermining the institution of slavery and eventually leading to its abolition in the 19th century.

The Industrial Revolution had a complex and multifaceted impact on the institution of slavery, human exploitation, and economic growth. While it fueled the expansion and intensification of slavery in colonial territories, it also contributed to the eventual decline of slavery as economic conditions and labor relations changed. Understanding the relationship between the Industrial Revolution, slavery, and economic development is essential for comprehending the historical roots of modern capitalism and the enduring legacies of exploitation and inequality within capitalist societies.

Chapter 2: Economic Exploitation

Economic exploitation within capitalism is a complex and multifaceted phenomenon that arises from the inherent power imbalances between different actors within the economic system. It involves the extraction of surplus value from workers by capitalists, resulting in unequal distribution of wealth, income, and power. Understanding economic exploitation within capitalism requires an exploration of its various forms, mechanisms, and consequences.

Exploring Modern Forms of Economic Coercion through Wage Labor and Exploitative Working Conditions

Exploring modern forms of economic coercion within capitalism unveils a complex landscape where wage labor and exploitative working conditions are prevalent, posing significant challenges to workers' rights, dignity, and well-being. In understanding these dynamics, it's essential to delve into the mechanisms, manifestations, and consequences of economic coercion in contemporary capitalist societies.

At the heart of modern economic coercion lies the relationship between workers and employers, characterized by unequal bargaining power and asymmetric information. While workers depend on employment for their livelihoods, capitalists control the means of production and resources, giving them significant leverage in setting wages, determining working conditions, and enforcing labor contracts. This power imbalance creates fertile ground for economic coercion, where workers are compelled to accept exploitative conditions out of necessity rather than choice.

One of the primary mechanisms of economic coercion in modern capitalism is the commodification of labor.

In capitalist economies, labor is treated as a commodity to be bought and sold in the market, subject to the laws of supply and demand. This commodification of labor gives employers the power to dictate the terms of employment, including wages, benefits, and working hours, often at the expense of workers' rights and well-being. Workers who are unable to find alternative employment opportunities may feel compelled to accept exploitative conditions out of fear of unemployment or economic insecurity.

Moreover, economic coercion within capitalism is perpetuated by structural factors such as globalization, deregulation, and the erosion of labor rights. Globalization has led to increased competition for jobs and downward pressure on wages, as companies seek to maximize profits by outsourcing production to low-wage countries with lax labor regulations. Deregulation of labor markets and weakening of labor unions have further diminished workers' bargaining power, allowing employers to impose exploitative working conditions with impunity.

Exploitative working conditions within capitalism manifest in various forms, including low wages, long hours, unsafe working conditions, and lack of job security. Many workers in capitalist economies are trapped in precarious employment arrangements, such as temporary contracts, part-time work, and gig economy jobs, which offer little stability or protection. Moreover, workers in industries such as agriculture, manufacturing, and service sectors often face hazardous conditions, inadequate safety measures, and lack of access to healthcare and social protections.

The consequences of exploitative working conditions within capitalism are profound and far-reaching, affecting workers' physical and mental health, quality of life, and overall well-being. Workers who are subjected to long hours, low wages, and unsafe working conditions are at increased risk of injury, illness, and stress-related disorders. Moreover, economic coercion can lead to social alienation, disenfranchisement, and loss of dignity, as workers are denied agency and autonomy in their employment.

Furthermore, exploitative working conditions within capitalism have broader implications for society as a whole, including income inequality, social polarization, and economic instability. As wealth and power become concentrated in the hands of a few, inequalities between rich and poor, employers and workers, become more pronounced, leading to social tensions and unrest. Moreover, exploitative working conditions can undermine economic productivity, innovation, and growth, as workers are demoralized, disengaged, and unable to reach their full potential.

Exploring modern forms of economic coercion within capitalism reveals a complex web of power dynamics, structural inequalities, and human exploitation. Wage labor and exploitative working conditions are pervasive features of contemporary capitalist societies, posing significant challenges to workers' rights, dignity, and well-being. Addressing economic coercion within capitalism requires structural changes to the economic system, including measures to strengthen labor rights, regulate working conditions, and promote economic justice for all.

The Effects of Capitalism on Worker Rights, Income Inequality, and Wealth Inequalities

The effects of capitalism on worker rights, income inequality, and wealth inequalities are profound and multifaceted, shaping the economic, social, and political landscape of contemporary societies. Understanding these effects requires an exploration of the mechanisms, manifestations, and consequences of capitalism's impact on workers and broader patterns of economic inequality.

Worker rights are fundamental to ensuring fair and equitable treatment in the workplace, including the right to fair wages, safe working conditions, collective bargaining, and protection from discrimination and exploitation. However, capitalism's emphasis on profit maximization and market competition often comes at the expense of worker rights, as employers seek to minimize labor costs and maximize productivity. This can lead to violations of labor rights, including wage theft, unsafe working conditions, and denial of workers' rights to organize and collectively bargain.

Income inequality refers to the unequal distribution of income among individuals or households within a society, often measured by indicators such as the Gini coefficient or the ratio of top earners' income to that of the bottom earners. Capitalism tends to exacerbate income inequality due to its inherent dynamics of wealth accumulation and concentration. In capitalist economies, individuals and corporations are driven by profit incentives, leading to unequal rewards for labor, investment, and entrepreneurship. As a result, high earners and capital owners capture a disproportionate share of the economic gains, while low-wage workers and marginalized communities struggle to make ends meet.

Wealth inequality, on the other hand, refers to the unequal distribution of assets and wealth among individuals or households, including property, stocks, bonds, and other financial assets. Capitalism's emphasis on private property rights and market competition can lead to the concentration of wealth in the hands of a few, as capitalists accumulate capital and assets through inheritance, investment, and business ownership. This concentration of wealth can perpetuate intergenerational inequality, as wealthy individuals pass down their assets to future generations, further entrenching disparities in economic power and opportunity.

These effects have profound social and economic consequences. In terms of worker rights, violations of labor rights can lead to exploitation, discrimination, and social injustice, undermining workers' dignity, health, and well-being. Moreover, income inequality can exacerbate social tensions and divisions within society, leading to social unrest, political polarization, and erosion of social cohesion. Wealth inequalities, meanwhile, can perpetuate intergenerational poverty and disadvantage, as marginalized communities lack access to resources, opportunities, and social mobility.

The effects of capitalism on worker rights, income inequality, and wealth inequalities are pervasive and far-reaching, shaping the economic, social, and political dynamics of contemporary societies. Addressing these inequalities requires structural changes to the economic system, including measures to strengthen labor rights, regulate corporate power, and promote economic justice for all. Moreover, addressing intersecting dimensions of inequality, including race, gender, and class, is essential for building more inclusive and equitable societies that prioritize human dignity, well-being, and social justice.

Globalization and the Abuse of Labor in Underdeveloped Nations

Globalization, as facilitated by capitalism, has transformed the dynamics of international trade, investment, and production, leading to both opportunities and challenges for workers in underdeveloped nations. While globalization has the potential to promote economic development and integration, it has also been associated with the abuse of labor rights and exploitation of workers in some parts of the world. Understanding the relationship between capitalism, globalization, and the abuse of labor in underdeveloped nations requires an examination of the mechanisms, consequences, and responses to these dynamics.

One of the primary mechanisms through which globalization contributes to the abuse of labor in underdeveloped nations is through the pursuit of profit maximization and cost-cutting strategies by multinational corporations (MNCs) and global supply chains. In search of cheap labor and lax regulations, MNCs often outsource production to underdeveloped nations where labor costs are low and labor protections are weak. This can lead to the exploitation of workers through long hours, low wages, unsafe working conditions, and denial of labor rights, including the right to organize and collectively bargain.

Moreover, globalization has intensified competition among countries and regions to attract foreign investment and compete in global markets, leading to a race to the bottom in labor standards and regulations. Underdeveloped nations may engage in deregulation and labor market flexibility to attract foreign investment, sacrificing labor rights and protections in the process. This can create a permissive environment for the abuse of labor, as employers exploit loopholes in labor laws and regulations to maximize profits at the expense of workers' well-being.

Furthermore, globalization has facilitated the fragmentation and outsourcing of production processes through global supply chains, where different stages of production are dispersed across multiple countries and regions. This can lead to increased complexity and opacity in supply chains, making it difficult to monitor and regulate labor conditions and ensure compliance with labor standards. Workers at the bottom of global supply chains, including those in subcontracted factories and informal sectors, are particularly vulnerable to exploitation and abuse, as they lack bargaining power and legal protections.

The consequences of globalization and the abuse of labor in underdeveloped nations are profound and far-reaching, affecting workers' rights, dignity, and well-being, as well as broader patterns of economic development and inequality. Workers who are subjected to exploitation and abuse often face physical and mental health risks, including injuries, illnesses, and stress-related disorders. Moreover, economic exploitation can perpetuate cycles of poverty and deprivation, as workers struggle to meet their basic needs and escape from poverty traps.

Furthermore, globalization and the abuse of labor in underdeveloped nations can have broader implications for economic development, social stability, and global governance. Exploitative labor practices can undermine efforts to achieve sustainable development goals, including poverty reduction, gender equality, and decent work for all. Moreover, social unrest, political instability, and labor protests may arise in response to labor exploitation, posing risks to social cohesion and political stability within countries and regions.

In response to the abuse of labor in underdeveloped nations, there have been efforts by governments, international organizations, civil society groups, and labor unions to promote labor rights, improve working conditions, and hold corporations accountable for their actions. Initiatives such as the International Labour Organization (ILO), Fair Labor Association (FLA), and Ethical Trading Initiative (ETI) seek to promote labor standards, corporate social responsibility, and ethical sourcing practices within global supply chains. Moreover, advocacy campaigns, consumer activism, and public pressure have led to increased awareness and scrutiny of labor conditions in underdeveloped nations, pushing for greater transparency, accountability, and respect for workers' rights.

The relationship between capitalism, globalization, and the abuse of labor in underdeveloped nations underscores the complex and contested nature of contemporary global capitalism. While globalization has the potential to promote economic development and integration, it also poses risks and challenges for workers in underdeveloped nations, who are vulnerable to exploitation and abuse in global supply chains. Addressing the abuse of labor requires collective action and coordinated efforts by governments, international organizations, corporations, and civil society to promote labor rights, improve working conditions, and ensure respect for human dignity and social justice in the global economy.

Chapter 3: Social Inequality: The Legacy of Slavery - Persistent Racial Injustice and Systemic Discrimination

Social inequality, particularly along racial lines, is deeply entrenched within capitalist societies, with historical legacies of slavery playing a significant role in perpetuating persistent racial injustice and systemic discrimination. Understanding the relationship between capitalism, social inequality, and racial injustice requires an examination of the historical roots, mechanisms, and consequences of these dynamics, as well as efforts to address and redress systemic inequalities.

The legacy of slavery in capitalist societies is a painful reminder of the deep-seated racial injustices and inequalities that continue to shape contemporary social and economic structures. Slavery, as an institution, was central to the economic development and wealth accumulation of capitalist economies, particularly in the Americas, where enslaved Africans were exploited for labor on plantations, mines, and other industries. The exploitation of enslaved labor contributed to the accumulation of wealth and power among white elites, while perpetuating racial hierarchies and inequalities that persist to this day.

Moreover, the abolition of slavery in the 19th century did not mark the end of racial injustice and discrimination within capitalist societies. Instead, racial hierarchies and inequalities were perpetuated and reinforced through other means, such as Jim Crow laws, segregation, and racial violence, which denied African Americans and other racial minorities equal rights and opportunities in education, employment, housing, and political participation. These discriminatory practices and policies created enduring patterns of social inequality, poverty, and marginalization that continue to shape racial dynamics within capitalist societies.

Furthermore, capitalism's emphasis on profit maximization and market competition can exacerbate racial inequalities and disparities in wealth, income, and access to resources. Racial minorities, particularly African Americans, face systemic barriers and discrimination in the labor market, including hiring biases, wage differentials, and occupational segregation, which limit their economic opportunities and mobility. Moreover, racial minorities are disproportionately represented in low-wage and precarious employment sectors, where they are vulnerable to exploitation, discrimination, and lack of labor protections.

The consequences of social inequality and racial injustice within capitalism are profound and far-reaching, affecting individuals, communities, and societies in various ways. Racial minorities, particularly African Americans, experience higher rates of poverty, unemployment, incarceration, and health disparities compared to their white counterparts. Moreover, racial inequality intersects with other dimensions of social inequality, including gender, class, and immigration status, further exacerbating disparities and exclusion within capitalist societies.

Efforts to address social inequality and racial injustice within capitalism require structural changes to the economic system, including measures to promote racial equity, economic justice, and social inclusion. This includes policies to address systemic racism and discrimination, such as affirmative action, anti-discrimination laws, and diversity initiatives, which seek to dismantle barriers to equal opportunity and promote inclusion and representation of racial minorities in all sectors of society.

Moreover, addressing social inequality within capitalism requires broader efforts to address economic disparities and promote shared prosperity for all members of society. This includes policies to reduce income inequality, such as progressive taxation, social safety nets, and living wage laws, which seek to redistribute wealth and resources to those most in need. Additionally, efforts to promote economic empowerment, community development, and asset-building among marginalized communities can help address the root causes of social inequality and create pathways to economic opportunity

The relationship between capitalism, social inequality, and racial injustice is a complex and multifaceted one, shaped by historical legacies, systemic discrimination, and structural inequalities. Addressing social inequality and racial injustice within capitalism requires collective action and political will to promote racial equity, economic justice, and social inclusion for all members of society.

Gender, Class, and Intersectional Identities in the Capitalist System

Social inequalities within capitalism intersect with various dimensions, including gender, class, and intersectional identities, creating complex and multidimensional patterns of privilege and disadvantage. Understanding the intersectionality of social inequalities requires an examination of how multiple axes of identity and oppression intersect and interact within capitalist societies.

Gender inequality is a pervasive and persistent feature of capitalist societies, rooted in historical and structural factors that privilege men over women in various spheres of life. In the workplace, women face systemic barriers and discrimination, including gender wage gaps, occupational segregation, and glass ceilings that limit their access to higher-paying and leadership positions. Moreover, women are disproportionately burdened with unpaid care work and domestic responsibilities, which further exacerbate economic inequalities and limit their participation in the labor market.

Class inequality, meanwhile, refers to disparities in wealth, income, and social status that arise from differential access to resources and opportunities within capitalist societies. Capitalism tends to concentrate wealth and power in the hands of a small elite, while relegating the majority of the population to lower socioeconomic positions. Working-class individuals and families often face economic insecurity, low wages, and limited access to social mobility, perpetuating cycles of poverty and disadvantage across generations.

Intersectionality, a concept developed by black feminist scholars, highlights the interconnectedness of multiple dimensions of identity, including race, gender, class, sexuality, and disability, in shaping individuals' experiences of oppression and privilege. Intersectional identities intersect and interact in complex ways, producing unique forms of discrimination and marginalization that cannot be understood through single-axis analyses. For example, women of color may face compounded forms of discrimination based on both their gender and race, leading to unique challenges and barriers in accessing employment, education, and healthcare.

Moreover, social inequalities within capitalism are reinforced and perpetuated through institutionalized systems of oppression and discrimination that operate at both the individual and structural levels. These systems include laws, policies, and practices that uphold patriarchal, capitalist, and white supremacist ideologies, privileging certain groups over others and perpetuating patterns of exclusion and marginalization. For example, discriminatory hiring practices, unequal access to education, and racial profiling in policing all contribute to the reproduction of social inequalities within capitalist societies.

The consequences of social inequalities within capitalism are profound and far-reaching, affecting individuals, families, and communities in various ways. Gender inequality, for example, contributes to women's economic insecurity, limited access to resources, and vulnerability to violence and exploitation. Class inequality perpetuates cycles of poverty and deprivation, limiting opportunities for upward mobility and social advancement. Intersectional identities further compound these inequalities, creating unique forms of marginalization and exclusion for individuals who occupy multiple marginalized identities.

Efforts to address social inequalities within capitalism require a multifaceted approach that addresses the root causes of oppression and discrimination while promoting equity, justice, and inclusion for all members of society. This includes policies and programs aimed at dismantling structural barriers to equality, such as affirmative action, anti-discrimination laws, and social welfare programs that provide support to marginalized communities. Moreover, efforts to promote diversity, equity, and inclusion in workplaces, schools, and other institutions can help create environments that are more accessible and welcoming to individuals from diverse backgrounds.

Furthermore, addressing social inequalities within capitalism requires a shift in cultural attitudes and beliefs that perpetuate stereotypes, biases, and prejudices based on race, gender, and other axes of identity. Education and awareness-raising initiatives can help challenge harmful stereotypes and promote empathy, understanding, and solidarity across different social groups. Additionally, grassroots organizing and social movements play a crucial role in advocating for social change and challenging systems of oppression and exploitation within capitalist societies.

Social inequalities within capitalism intersect with multiple dimensions of identity, including gender, class, and intersectional identities, creating complex and multidimensional patterns of privilege and disadvantage. Addressing these inequalities requires a comprehensive and intersectional approach that tackles the root causes of oppression and discrimination while promoting equity, justice, and inclusion for all members of society. By challenging systems of oppression and working towards a more just and equitable world, we can create a society where everyone has the opportunity to thrive and flourish, regardless of their social identities.

Capitalism, Race, and Social Stratification: Examining the Intersectionality of Oppression

Social inequalities within capitalism intersect with various dimensions of identity, including race, creating complex systems of privilege and oppression that shape individuals' experiences and opportunities within society. Understanding the intersectionality of capitalism, race, and social stratification requires an examination of historical legacies, structural dynamics, and contemporary manifestations of racial inequality within capitalist societies.

Race has been a central organizing principle of social stratification within capitalist societies, with racial hierarchies and inequalities deeply embedded in economic, political, and cultural structures. Historically, capitalism has been intertwined with processes of colonization, slavery, and racial exploitation, which have shaped the distribution of wealth, power, and resources along racial lines. The legacy of slavery, segregation, and racial discrimination continues to inform patterns of racial inequality and social stratification in contemporary capitalist societies.

Capitalism has played a significant role in shaping racial inequalities through processes of racialization, which involve the categorization and construction of racial identities based on perceived differences in physical appearance, culture, and ancestry. Racialized groups are often subjected to systemic discrimination and exclusion within capitalist societies, limiting their access to economic opportunities, political representation, and social mobility. Moreover, capitalism has historically relied on racialized labor, such as enslaved Africans in the Americas, to fuel economic growth and accumulation, perpetuating racial hierarchies and inequalities.

Intersectionality, a concept developed by black feminist scholars, highlights the interconnectedness of race, gender, class, and other dimensions of identity in shaping individuals' experiences of oppression and privilege. Intersectional approaches to understanding social inequalities recognize that individuals occupy multiple social positions simultaneously and that these intersecting identities interact in complex ways to produce unique forms of discrimination and marginalization. For example, black women may experience compounded forms of oppression based on both their race and gender, facing discrimination and exclusion in both spheres of life.

Moreover, capitalism's emphasis on profit maximization and market competition can exacerbate racial inequalities by perpetuating systems of exploitation and exclusion. Racialized groups, particularly black and indigenous communities, are disproportionately represented in low-wage and precarious employment sectors, where they are vulnerable to exploitation, discrimination, and lack of labor protections. Moreover, racial minorities face systemic barriers to accessing education, housing, healthcare, and other resources, further perpetuating patterns of racial inequality and social stratification.

The consequences of capitalism, race, and social stratification are profound and far-reaching, affecting individuals, families, and communities in various ways. Racial inequalities contribute to disparities in wealth, income, education, health, and criminal justice outcomes, perpetuating cycles of poverty, deprivation, and marginalization for racialized groups. Moreover, racial discrimination and exclusion undermine social cohesion, trust, and solidarity within society, leading to social tensions, conflict, and unrest.

Efforts to address racial inequalities within capitalism require a multifaceted approach that addresses the root causes of racial oppression and discrimination while promoting racial equity, justice, and inclusion for all members of society. This includes policies and programs aimed at dismantling structural barriers to equality, such as affirmative action, anti-discrimination laws, and reparations for historical injustices. Moreover, efforts to promote diversity, equity, and inclusion in workplaces, schools, and other institutions can help create environments that are more accessible and welcoming to individuals from racially marginalized communities.

Furthermore, addressing racial inequalities within capitalism requires a shift in cultural attitudes and beliefs that perpetuate stereotypes, biases, and prejudices based on race. Education and awareness-raising initiatives can help challenge harmful stereotypes and promote empathy, understanding, and solidarity across racial lines. Additionally, grassroots organizing and social movements play a crucial role in advocating for racial justice and challenging systems of oppression and exploitation within capitalist societies.

In summary, the intersectionality of capitalism, race, and social stratification underscores the complex and multifaceted nature of racial inequality within contemporary societies. Understanding and addressing racial inequalities within capitalism requires a comprehensive and intersectional approach that tackles the root causes of racial oppression and discrimination while promoting racial equity, justice, and inclusion for all members of society. By challenging systems of racial oppression and working towards a more just and equitable world, we can create a society where everyone has the opportunity to thrive and flourish, regardless of their race or ethnicity.

Read more about freedom in <u>Freedom In Capitalism</u>

Chapter 4: Environmental Degradation

Environmental degradation within capitalism is a pressing global concern that arises from the prioritization of profit maximization and economic growth over ecological sustainability and environmental protection. Understanding the relationship between capitalism and environmental degradation requires an examination of the structural dynamics, incentives, and consequences of capitalist production and consumption patterns on the natural environment.

One of the key drivers of environmental degradation within capitalism is the relentless pursuit of economic growth and expansion, which often comes at the expense of natural resources, ecosystems, and biodiversity. Capitalist economies rely on the extraction and exploitation of natural resources, such as fossil fuels, minerals, and timber, to fuel production and consumption processes, leading to deforestation, habitat destruction, and depletion of finite resources.

Furthermore, capitalism's reliance on consumerism and mass consumption exacerbates environmental degradation by promoting wasteful and unsustainable patterns of production and consumption. Advertising, marketing, and consumer culture encourage individuals to constantly consume and dispose of goods and services, leading to overconsumption, resource depletion, and waste generation. This "throwaway culture" perpetuates a linear model of production and consumption, where goods are produced, consumed, and discarded at an unsustainable rate, leading to environmental degradation and ecological overshoot.

The consequences of environmental degradation within capitalism are profound and far-reaching, affecting ecosystems, biodiversity, and human well-being on a global scale. Climate change, driven by greenhouse gas emissions from burning fossil fuels, deforestation, and industrial activities, poses existential threats to ecosystems, communities, and future generations. Moreover, environmental degradation exacerbates social inequalities and injustices, as marginalized communities and vulnerable populations bear the brunt of environmental pollution, contamination, and climate impacts.

Efforts to address environmental degradation within capitalism require systemic changes to the economic system, including measures to internalize environmental costs, regulate polluting industries, and promote sustainable production and consumption practices. This includes implementing policies such as carbon pricing, pollution taxes, and environmental regulations that incentivize corporations to reduce their environmental footprint and invest in clean technologies and renewable energy sources.

Moreover, transitioning to a more sustainable and regenerative economy requires reimagining the role of government, business, and civil society in promoting environmental stewardship and ecological resilience. This includes investing in green infrastructure, renewable energy, and ecosystem restoration projects that create jobs, stimulate economic growth, and protect natural resources and ecosystems. Additionally, promoting environmental justice and equitable access to clean air, water, and land is essential for addressing environmental inequalities and ensuring that all communities have the right to a healthy and sustainable environment.

Environmental degradation within capitalism is a systemic and complex issue that arises from the prioritization of profit maximization and economic growth over ecological sustainability and environmental protection. Addressing environmental degradation requires transformative changes to the economic system, including internalizing environmental costs, regulating polluting industries, and promoting sustainable production and consumption practices. By reimagining our relationship with the natural world and prioritizing environmental stewardship and ecological resilience, we can create a more sustainable and equitable future for all.

Capitalism and the exploitation of Natural Resources: Environmental Destruction in the Pursuit of Profit

Capitalism's relationship with the exploitation of natural resources is complex, marked by a tension between economic growth and environmental conservation. Within capitalist economies, natural resources are often treated as commodities to be exploited for profit, leading to environmental destruction and degradation in the pursuit of economic gain. Understanding the dynamics of capitalism and the exploitation of natural resources requires an examination of the mechanisms, incentives, and consequences of capitalist production and consumption patterns on the environment.

Moreover, capitalism's reliance on economic growth and expansion exacerbates the pressure on natural resources, as industries compete for access to scarce resources and seek to capitalize on emerging markets and opportunities. This can lead to the intensification of extractive industries, such as mining, drilling, and logging, which have significant environmental footprints and ecological consequences. Furthermore, globalization and international trade facilitate the global exploitation of natural resources, as corporations seek to exploit resources in developing countries with lax environmental regulations and labor standards.

The consequences of the exploitation of natural resources within capitalism are profound and far-reaching, affecting ecosystems, biodiversity, and human well-being on a global scale. Deforestation, driven by logging and agricultural expansion, leads to loss of habitat, soil erosion, and disruption of ecosystem services, such as carbon sequestration and water regulation. Mining activities, meanwhile, result in soil and water contamination, deforestation, and displacement of indigenous communities, causing irreversible damage to ecosystems and threatening local

livelihoods.

Furthermore, the extraction and burning of fossil fuels, such as coal, oil, and natural gas, are major contributors to climate change, as they release greenhouse gases into the atmosphere, leading to global warming and environmental instability. Climate change poses significant risks to ecosystems, communities, and economies, including more frequent and severe weather events, rising sea levels, and disruptions to food and water supplies. Moreover, marginalized communities and vulnerable populations, particularly in developing countries, bear the brunt of the impacts of environmental destruction and climate change, exacerbating social inequalities and injustices.

Efforts to address the exploitation of natural resources within capitalism require systemic changes to the economic system, including measures to internalize environmental costs, regulate polluting industries, and promote sustainable production and consumption practices. This includes implementing policies such as carbon pricing, pollution taxes, and environmental regulations that incentivize corporations to reduce their environmental footprint and invest in clean technologies and renewable energy sources.

Moreover, transitioning to a more sustainable and regenerative economy requires reimagining the role of government, business, and civil society in promoting environmental stewardship and ecological resilience. This includes investing in green infrastructure, renewable energy, and ecosystem restoration projects that create jobs, stimulate economic growth, and protect natural resources and ecosystems. Additionally, promoting environmental justice and equitable access to clean air, water, and land is essential for addressing environmental inequalities and ensuring that all communities have the right to a healthy and sustainable environment.

Capitalism's pursuit of profit and economic growth often comes at the expense of environmental destruction and degradation, as natural resources are exploited and depleted for short-term gains. Addressing the exploitation of natural resources within capitalism requires transformative changes to the economic system, including internalizing environmental costs, regulating polluting industries, and promoting sustainable production and consumption practices. By prioritizing environmental stewardship and ecological resilience, we can create a more sustainable and equitable future for all, where natural resources are protected and preserved for future generations.

The Real Cost of Capitalist Growth: Climate Change, Pollution, and Ecological Crisis

The real cost of capitalist growth extends far beyond economic metrics, encompassing a range of environmental and social consequences that have profound implications for the planet and its inhabitants. Climate change, pollution, and ecological degradation are among the most pressing challenges associated with capitalist growth, highlighting the unsustainable nature of current production and consumption patterns.

Climate change, driven primarily by the burning of fossil fuels and deforestation, poses existential threats to ecosystems, communities, and economies worldwide. Capitalist economies rely heavily on fossil fuels such as coal, oil, and natural gas for energy production, transportation, and industrial processes, releasing greenhouse gases into the atmosphere and causing global warming. This leads to a range of climate impacts, including more frequent and severe heatwaves, droughts, storms, and rising sea levels, which pose risks to human health, food security, and infrastructure.

Moreover, climate change exacerbates existing social inequalities and injustices, disproportionately affecting marginalized communities and vulnerable populations who lack the resources and resilience to adapt to environmental changes. Developing countries, in particular, bear the brunt of climate impacts, as they face challenges such as food insecurity, water scarcity, and displacement due to extreme weather events and environmental degradation. Additionally, indigenous peoples and frontline communities are often disproportionately affected by extractive industries and environmental pollution, further exacerbating social disparities and injustices.

Pollution, another consequence of capitalist growth, poses significant risks to human health, ecosystems, and biodiversity. Industrial activities such as manufacturing, mining, and agriculture produce harmful pollutants and waste, contaminating air, water, and soil and causing a range of adverse health effects, including respiratory diseases, cancer, and neurological disorders. Moreover, pollution disproportionately affects marginalized communities and low-income populations, who are more likely to live in areas with high levels of pollution and lack access to clean air, water, and sanitation.

Furthermore, capitalist economies generate vast amounts of waste and consumption, leading to resource depletion, environmental degradation, and loss of biodiversity. The linear model of production and consumption, where goods are produced, consumed, and discarded at an unsustainable rate, leads to overconsumption, waste generation, and depletion of finite resources. This results in the degradation of ecosystems, loss of habitat, and decline in biodiversity, threatening the long-term health and resilience of ecosystems and the services they provide to society.

Additionally, the pursuit of capitalist growth often comes at the expense of indigenous lands, cultures, and traditional livelihoods, as extractive industries and large-scale development projects encroach upon indigenous territories and undermine indigenous rights and sovereignty. Indigenous peoples, who are often the stewards of some of the world's most biodiverse and ecologically sensitive areas, face threats such as land grabbing, deforestation, and displacement, further exacerbating social inequalities and injustices.

Efforts to address the real cost of capitalist growth require transformative changes to the economic system, including measures to promote sustainability, resilience, and social justice. This includes transitioning to renewable energy sources, such as solar, wind, and hydroelectric power, and phasing out fossil fuel subsidies and investments. Moreover, promoting sustainable agriculture, land use, and resource management practices can help reduce pollution, protect ecosystems, and enhance resilience to environmental changes.

Furthermore, regulating polluting industries, implementing pollution control measures, and enforcing environmental regulations are essential for protecting human health and the environment from harmful pollutants and waste. Additionally, investing in clean technologies, green infrastructure, and circular economy initiatives can help reduce resource consumption, minimize waste generation, and promote sustainable production and consumption patterns.

Moreover, promoting environmental justice and equitable access to resources and opportunities is essential for addressing social inequalities and injustices exacerbated by capitalist growth. This includes supporting frontline communities, indigenous peoples, and marginalized populations in their efforts to protect their lands, cultures, and livelihoods from environmental degradation and exploitation. Additionally, fostering partnerships and collaborations between governments, businesses, civil society organizations, and indigenous peoples can help build resilience, promote sustainable development, and address the root causes of environmental and social injustices.

The real cost of capitalist growth extends beyond economic indicators, encompassing a range of environmental and social consequences that pose significant risks to ecosystems, communities, and future generations. Addressing the real cost of capitalist growth requires transformative changes to the economic system, including promoting sustainability, resilience, and social justice. By prioritizing environmental protection, social equity, and human well-being, we can create a more sustainable and equitable future for all.

Environmental Justice and the Battle Against Corporate Greed

Environmental justice, a concept rooted in principles of equity, fairness, and democracy, stands as a counterforce against the negative impacts of capitalism on the environment and marginalized communities. Capitalism's relentless pursuit of profit often comes at the expense of environmental degradation and social injustice, disproportionately affecting vulnerable populations and exacerbating inequalities. The battle against corporate greed and environmental injustice underscores the need for systemic change and collective action to address the root causes of environmental degradation and promote social and environmental justice.

One of the central challenges of capitalism is the concentration of wealth and power in the hands of corporations and the wealthy elite, who wield significant influence over political and economic decision-making processes. This enables corporations to prioritize profit maximization over environmental protection and social welfare, leading to the exploitation of natural resources, pollution, and environmental degradation. Environmental justice movements seek to challenge corporate greed and hold corporations accountable for their actions, advocating for greater transparency, accountability, and democratic control over decision-making processes.

Moreover, capitalism's reliance on fossil fuels and extractive industries exacerbates environmental injustices and contributes to climate change, which disproportionately affects marginalized communities and vulnerable populations. Frontline communities, including indigenous peoples, people of color, and low-income communities, are often disproportionately impacted by environmental pollution, contamination, and climate impacts, as they are more likely to live in areas with high levels of pollution and lack access to resources and resilience to environmental changes.

Furthermore, capitalism's emphasis on economic growth and expansion perpetuates patterns of environmental racism and discrimination, as corporations target marginalized communities and low-income neighborhoods for the siting of polluting industries and waste disposal facilities. This leads to environmental injustices such as toxic exposure, health disparities, and loss of land and livelihoods, further exacerbating social inequalities and injustices.

The battle against corporate greed and environmental injustice requires a multifaceted approach that addresses the structural drivers of inequality and environmental degradation within capitalist societies. This includes advocating for policies and regulations that promote environmental protection, social equity, and democratic governance, such as stricter pollution controls, environmental impact assessments, and community rights to participate in decision-making processes.

Moreover, promoting environmental justice requires centering the voices and experiences of frontline communities and marginalized populations in decision-making processes, ensuring that their concerns and priorities are taken into account in policy development and implementation. This includes supporting grassroots organizing, community-based initiatives, and indigenous-led movements that empower communities to advocate for their rights and hold corporations and governments accountable for their actions.

Additionally, fostering partnerships and collaborations between governments, businesses, civil society organizations, and communities can help build alliances and coalitions for environmental justice, mobilizing collective action and resources to address the root causes of environmental degradation and social injustice. This includes promoting sustainable development, renewable energy, and green jobs initiatives that create opportunities for economic empowerment and community resilience while protecting the environment and promoting social equity.

Furthermore, promoting environmental justice requires challenging the dominant narratives and ideologies that prioritize economic growth and corporate profits over human rights, environmental protection, and social welfare. This includes raising awareness, building solidarity, and advocating for transformative change at local, national, and global levels, fostering a culture of environmental responsibility, social justice, and solidarity among individuals, communities, and institutions.

The battle against corporate greed and environmental injustice is a fundamental struggle for social and environmental justice within capitalist societies. Addressing the root causes of environmental degradation and promoting social equity requires challenging the power dynamics and structural inequalities inherent in capitalism, while advocating for policies and practices that prioritize environmental protection, human rights, and community well-being. By mobilizing collective action and building alliances for environmental justice, we can create a more sustainable, equitable, and democratic future for all.

Related book by Greg V. Jack

Freedom In Capitalism

Chapter 5: Corporate Influence and Political Power

Corporate influence and political power are central issues in the critique of capitalism, highlighting the ways in which economic interests can shape and distort democratic processes and public policy. In capitalist societies, corporations wield significant power and influence over political decision-making, often at the expense of the public interest and democratic accountability. Understanding the relationship between capitalism, corporate influence, and political power requires an examination of the mechanisms, incentives, and consequences of corporate lobbying, campaign finance, and regulatory capture within political systems.

Corporate lobbying, in particular, is a common strategy employed by corporations to influence legislative and regulatory processes, often through direct advocacy, campaign contributions, and the funding of think tanks and advocacy groups. Lobbying allows corporations to shape public policy to their advantage, influencing everything from tax policy and environmental regulations to healthcare reform and consumer protection laws. Moreover, corporate lobbying often operates behind closed doors, away from public scrutiny, raising concerns about transparency, accountability,

Furthermore, regulatory capture, a phenomenon where regulatory agencies become dominated by the industries they are supposed to regulate, further entrenches corporate influence over political decision-making. Regulatory agencies tasked with overseeing industries such as banking, energy, and pharmaceuticals often become captured by industry interests, leading to lax enforcement, weak regulations, and industry-friendly policies that prioritize corporate profits over public health, safety, and welfare.

Corporate Capitalism and Democracy's Decline: The Politics of Money's Influence Regulatory Capture and the Subversion of Public Interest

Corporate capitalism and democracy's decline are intertwined phenomena that highlight the erosion of democratic governance and the subversion of public interest in the face of corporate power and influence. In capitalist societies, the concentration of wealth and power in the hands of corporations and the wealthy elite undermines democratic principles and processes, leading to regulatory capture, the politics of money's influence, and the prioritization of corporate interests over the common good. Understanding the dynamics of corporate capitalism and democracy's decline requires an examination of the mechanisms, incentives, and consequences of corporate influence on political decision-making and public policy.

Campaign finance, in particular, plays a significant role in the politics of money's influence, allowing corporations and wealthy individuals to pour money into political campaigns and elections in exchange for access and influence over elected officials and policymakers. The influence of money in politics undermines the principle of political equality and gives undue influence to wealthy donors and special interest groups, distorting democratic processes and eroding public trust in government institutions. Moreover, revolving door politics, where individuals move between government positions and private-sector jobs, further blurs the lines between corporate interests and government officials, creating conflicts of interest and undermining public trust in the integrity of the political process.

The consequences of corporate capitalism and democracy's decline are profound and far-reaching, affecting the integrity of democratic governance, the accountability of elected officials, and the ability of governments to address pressing social and environmental challenges. Corporate influence and regulatory capture undermine efforts to address systemic issues such as income inequality, climate change, and social injustice, perpetuating inequalities and injustices within society. Moreover, the erosion of democratic principles and processes undermines the legitimacy of government institutions and fosters disillusionment and distrust among the public, threatening the stability and viability of democratic governance.

Efforts to address corporate capitalism and democracy's decline require systemic changes to the political system, including measures to limit the influence of money in politics, strengthen transparency and accountability mechanisms, and promote democratic governance. This includes campaign finance reform, such as public financing of elections and stricter limits on campaign contributions, to reduce the influence of wealthy donors and special interest groups in political campaigns and elections. Moreover, efforts to address regulatory capture require strengthening regulatory agencies, enhancing their independence, and increasing transparency and accountability in decision-making processes. This includes implementing conflict-of-interest rules, revolving door restrictions, and whistleblower protections to prevent undue industry influence and promote the public interest in regulatory decision-making.

Furthermore, promoting corporate accountability and responsible business practices is essential for addressing corporate influence and ensuring that corporations act in the public interest. This includes promoting transparency, disclosure, and stakeholder engagement in corporate governance, as well as holding corporations accountable for their social, environmental, and human rights impacts through regulatory enforcement, litigation, and shareholder activism. By promoting transparency, accountability, and democratic governance, we can help ensure that political decision-making serves the public interest and advances the common good, thereby strengthening democracy and mitigating the harmful effects of corporate capitalism.

How Corporations Influence Government Policy - Fighting for Economic Justice and Grassroots Movements' Resistance to Corporate Power

The influence of corporations on government policy is a critical aspect of the disadvantages associated with capitalism, often resulting in policies that prioritize corporate interests over the public good. Understanding how corporations wield power in shaping government policies requires examining the mechanisms through which they exert influence, the consequences of their actions, and strategies for challenging corporate dominance to fight for economic justice through grassroots movements.

Campaign contributions are another means through which corporations exert influence on government policy, providing financial support to political candidates and parties in exchange for access and influence over the policymaking process. Campaign finance laws in many countries allow corporations to donate unlimited amounts of money to political campaigns, leading to concerns about the influence of money in politics and the potential for corruption and undue influence over elected officials. This enables corporations to effectively buy access and influence in the political arena, distorting democratic processes and undermining public trust in government institutions.

Moreover, the revolving door between the private sector and government positions creates conflicts of interest and opportunities for regulatory capture, as individuals move between roles in government and industry, blurring the lines between corporate interests and public service. Former government officials often leverage their connections and insider knowledge to secure lucrative positions in the private sector, where they advocate for policies that benefit their former employers or clients. This phenomenon undermines the independence and integrity of government institutions, eroding public trust and confidence in the impartiality of the policymaking process.

The consequences of corporate influence on government policy are far-reaching and often detrimental to the public interest, leading to policies that prioritize corporate profits over the well-being of people and the planet. Deregulation, tax cuts for the wealthy and corporations, and subsidies for industries such as fossil fuels and agribusiness perpetuate inequalities, exacerbate environmental degradation, and undermine social welfare programs. Moreover, corporate-friendly policies often weaken labor rights, consumer protections, and environmental regulations, leaving workers, consumers, and communities vulnerable to exploitation, harm, and abuse.

Fighting for economic justice and challenging corporate influence on government policy requires grassroots movements and collective action to hold corporations and policymakers accountable and advocate for policies that prioritize the needs and interests of the public. Grassroots movements, such as labor unions, environmental organizations, and community groups, play a crucial role in mobilizing people power and advocating for systemic change to address the root causes of economic inequality, corporate power, and political corruption.

One strategy for challenging corporate influence on government policy is through grassroots organizing and advocacy campaigns that raise awareness, build solidarity, and mobilize public support for progressive policies and reforms. Grassroots movements can pressure policymakers to enact policies that promote economic justice, such as raising the minimum wage, strengthening labor rights, and implementing progressive taxation to ensure that corporations and the wealthy pay their fair share.

Furthermore, grassroots movements can push for campaign finance reform to reduce the influence of money in politics and promote transparency, accountability, and democratic governance. This includes advocating for measures such as public financing of elections, strict limits on campaign contributions, and disclosure requirements for political spending to ensure that elections are free, fair, and accessible to all citizens, not just wealthy donors and special interest groups.

Additionally, grassroots movements can challenge corporate power and influence through direct action, civil disobedience, and boycotts, targeting corporations and industries that engage in unethical or harmful practices. By organizing protests, boycotts, and divestment campaigns, grassroots movements can pressure corporations to change their behavior and adopt more responsible and sustainable business practices that respect human rights, environmental sustainability, and social justice.

The influence of corporations on government policy is a significant disadvantage of capitalism, often resulting in policies that prioritize corporate interests over the public good. Challenging corporate influence and fighting for economic justice require grassroots movements and collective action to hold corporations and policymakers accountable and advocate for policies that promote the well-being of people and the planet. By organizing, mobilizing, and advocating for progressive policies and reforms, grassroots movements can help build a more just, equitable, and sustainable society where the needs and interests of the many are prioritized over the profits of the few.

Chapter 6: The Role of Activism and Social Movements in Challenging Capitalist Oppression

The role of activism and social movements in challenging capitalist oppression is essential for fostering social change, promoting justice, and advancing the interests of marginalized communities. Activism serves as a catalyst for challenging the status quo, raising awareness about systemic injustices, and mobilizing people's power to demand transformative reforms. Social movements, characterized by collective action and solidarity, play a crucial role in challenging capitalist oppression by organizing protests, advocating for policy change, and building grassroots power to address the root causes of inequality, exploitation, and injustice.

One of the primary functions of activism and social movements is to amplify the voices and experiences of marginalized communities and challenge dominant narratives and power structures that perpetuate oppression and inequality within capitalist societies. By centering the perspectives and struggles of marginalized groups, including people of color, indigenous peoples, women, and workers, social movements bring attention to the intersecting forms of oppression and discrimination that shape people's lives and experiences.

Moreover, activism and social movements provide a platform for marginalized communities to articulate their demands, assert their rights, and mobilize collective action to challenge capitalist oppression and demand justice. By organizing protests, marches, rallies, and direct actions, social movements create visibility and public pressure on decision-makers and power holders to address systemic issues such as racism, sexism, economic inequality, and environmental degradation.

Furthermore, activism and social movements serve as vehicles for solidarity and mutual aid, fostering connections and building alliances across different communities, movements, and struggles. By forging solidarity and building coalitions, social movements strengthen their collective power and amplify their impact, challenging capitalist oppression and advocating for transformative change at local, national, and global levels.

One of the key strategies of activism and social movements in challenging capitalist oppression is through grassroots organizing and community empowerment. Grassroots organizing involves building power from the bottom up, mobilizing people at the local level to address their own needs and concerns, and challenging the structures of power and privilege that perpetuate inequality and injustice. By empowering communities to take collective action and advocate for their rights, grassroots organizing builds resilience, fosters solidarity, and creates spaces for people to envision and create alternative systems based on principles of justice, equity, and democracy.

Moreover, activism and social movements play a crucial role in shaping public discourse and influencing political agendas, challenging dominant narratives and ideologies that justify capitalist exploitation and oppression. By raising awareness, educating the public, and challenging misinformation and propaganda, social movements create opportunities for critical reflection, dialogue, and collective action to challenge capitalist hegemony and promote alternative visions of society based on principles of solidarity, cooperation, and justice.

Additionally, activism and social movements leverage a variety of tactics and strategies to challenge capitalist oppression, including direct action, civil disobedience, advocacy campaigns, legal challenges, and cultural interventions. These tactics disrupt business as usual, challenge the legitimacy of unjust systems and institutions, and create space for alternative voices and perspectives to be heard and amplified.

Furthermore, activism and social movements play a crucial role in holding corporations and governments accountable for their actions and advocating for policies and practices that promote social, economic, and environmental justice. By organizing boycotts, divestment campaigns, and shareholder activism, social movements pressure corporations to adopt more responsible and sustainable business practices that respect human rights, environmental sustainability, and social justice. Additionally, by lobbying policymakers, advocating for legislative reforms, and engaging in electoral politics, social movements seek to influence public policy and institutional change to address systemic issues such as economic inequality, racial injustice, and environmental degradation.

Moreover, activism and social movements challenge the commodification and exploitation of people and the planet under capitalism by advocating for alternative models of economic organization and resource distribution that prioritize the well-being of communities and ecosystems over corporate profits. By promoting principles of solidarity, cooperation, and mutual aid, social movements envision and create alternative economic systems based on principles of equity, sustainability, and democratic control.

The role of activism and social movements in challenging capitalist oppression is vital for fostering social change, promoting justice, and advancing the interests of marginalized communities. By organizing collective action, challenging dominant narratives, and advocating for policy change, social movements create opportunities for transformative change and build power from the bottom up to challenge capitalist hegemony and create a more just, equitable, and sustainable world for all.

Intersectional Approaches to Social Justice

Intersectionality is a critical framework for understanding and addressing the complexities of social justice issues within capitalist oppression. It recognizes that individuals' identities and experiences are shaped by multiple intersecting axes of oppression, including race, gender, class, sexuality, disability, and other social categories. In the context of activism and social movements, intersectional approaches to social justice emphasize the interconnectedness of various forms of oppression and advocate for strategies that address the unique experiences and needs of marginalized communities.

One key aspect of intersectional approaches to social justice is recognizing the ways in which different forms of oppression intersect and compound to produce unique experiences of marginalization and discrimination. For example, a Black woman may experience racism, sexism, and classism simultaneously, resulting in distinct forms of oppression that cannot be adequately addressed by focusing solely on race or gender alone. By understanding the intersectional nature of oppression, activists and social movements can develop more holistic and inclusive strategies that center the experiences and needs of marginalized communities.

Moreover, intersectional approaches to social justice emphasize the importance of centering the voices and leadership of those most directly affected by oppression. This involves recognizing the expertise and knowledge of marginalized communities and ensuring that they have a meaningful role in shaping the priorities, strategies, and decision-making processes of social movements. By centering the experiences and leadership of marginalized communities, intersectional approaches to social justice promote solidarity, accountability, and empowerment within activist movements.

Additionally, intersectional approaches to social justice highlight the interconnectedness of struggles for liberation and the importance of building alliances and solidarity across different movements and struggles. Recognizing that capitalism exploits and oppresses people along multiple axes of identity, intersectional approaches advocate for solidarity between movements for racial justice, gender equality, economic justice, environmental justice, and other social justice causes. By building bridges between different movements and amplifying shared goals and values, intersectional approaches to social justice strengthen collective power and create opportunities for transformative change.

Furthermore, intersectional approaches to social justice challenge essentialist and single-issue frameworks that prioritize one form of oppression over others or overlook the interconnectedness of various forms of oppression. Instead, intersectional approaches recognize the complexity and fluidity of identity and advocate for inclusive and intersectional analyses that consider how different forms of oppression intersect and shape individuals' experiences. By challenging essentialism and embracing intersectionality, activists and social movements can develop more nuanced and effective strategies for addressing systemic injustice and inequality.

Moreover, intersectional approaches to social justice highlight the importance of addressing structural and systemic factors that perpetuate oppression and inequality within capitalist societies. This involves challenging institutionalized forms of discrimination, such as racism, sexism, ableism, and homophobia, and advocating for policies and practices that promote equity, inclusion, and social justice. By addressing the root causes of oppression and inequality, intersectional approaches seek to create systemic change that benefits all members of society, particularly those who are most marginalized and vulnerable.

In conclusion, intersectional approaches to social justice play a crucial role in addressing capitalist oppression by recognizing the intersecting axes of oppression that shape individuals' experiences and advocating for strategies that center the voices and leadership of marginalized communities. By embracing intersectionality, activists and social movements can develop more holistic, inclusive, and effective strategies for challenging systemic injustice and inequality within capitalist societies. By building alliances, challenging essentialism, and addressing systemic factors that perpetuate oppression, intersectional approaches to social justice strengthen collective power and create opportunities for transformative change.

Leveraging Technology and Social Media

Leveraging technology and social media has become increasingly important for activism and social movements in challenging capitalist oppression. In the digital age, technology and social media platforms offer powerful tools for organizing, mobilizing, and amplifying voices, allowing activists to reach wider audiences, coordinate actions, and challenge dominant narratives. By harnessing the potential of technology and social media, activists and social movements can overcome barriers to communication, build solidarity, and mobilize collective action to address systemic injustices within capitalist societies.

Moreover, technology and social media platforms enable activists to organize and coordinate actions more efficiently and effectively. Online platforms facilitate real-time communication and collaboration among activists, allowing them to coordinate protests, rallies, and direct actions, share resources and information, and strategize tactics for challenging capitalist oppression. Additionally, crowdfunding platforms provide opportunities for grassroots fundraising and resource mobilization, enabling activists to finance their campaigns and sustain their efforts over the long term.

Furthermore, technology and social media platforms provide a platform for marginalized communities to share their stories, amplify their voices, and challenge dominant narratives that perpetuate oppression and inequality. By centering the voices and experiences of those most directly affected by capitalist oppression, social media platforms empower marginalized communities to reclaim their narratives, challenge stereotypes, and advocate for their rights and dignity. Additionally, online platforms such as blogs, podcasts, and online forums provide spaces for critical dialogue, education, and consciousness-raising on issues related to capitalism, oppression, and social justice.

Additionally, technology and social media platforms can serve as tools for documenting and exposing human rights abuses, corporate malfeasance, and environmental destruction perpetrated by capitalist institutions. Activists can use smartphones, cameras, and live streaming tools to capture and share evidence of injustice and wrongdoing, hold perpetrators accountable, and mobilize public pressure for accountability and reform. Moreover, digital advocacy campaigns such as online petitions, email campaigns, and social media boycotts can exert pressure on corporations, governments, and other power holders to change their policies and practices in response to public outcry.

Despite their potential benefits, it is essential to acknowledge the limitations and challenges associated with leveraging technology and social media for activism. The digital divide, for example, exacerbates inequalities in access to technology and internet connectivity, limiting the ability of marginalized communities to participate fully in online activism. Moreover, social media platforms are often subject to censorship, surveillance, and algorithmic biases that can restrict the reach and impact of activist content and amplify harmful narratives and misinformation. Additionally, the commodification of social media platforms by capitalist corporations raises concerns about data privacy, surveillance capitalism, and the commercialization of activism.

Leveraging technology and social media has become a vital strategy for activism and social movements in challenging capitalist oppression. By harnessing the power of digital tools and online platforms, activists can reach wider audiences, coordinate actions, amplify voices, and mobilize collective action to address systemic injustices within capitalist societies. While technology and social media offer unprecedented opportunities for activism, it is essential to recognize their limitations and challenges and work towards creating more inclusive, equitable, and accountable digital spaces for social justice activism.

Conclusion

In the closing pages of "Is Capitalism Slavery?" it becomes evident that the question posed in the title is not merely rhetorical but serves as a profound call to action. Throughout this exploration of capitalism's intricacies, injustices, and contradictions, one overarching theme emerges: the undeniable parallels between the exploitation inherent in capitalist systems and the historical abomination of slavery.

The journey through these pages has illuminated the myriad ways in which capitalism perpetuates systems of oppression, inequality, and exploitation. From the commodification of labor to the concentration of wealth and power in the hands of the few, the similarities between capitalist exploitation and historical slavery are striking. Just as enslaved individuals were treated as mere commodities, bought and sold for profit, so too are workers under capitalism subjected to dehumanizing conditions and reduced to the status of expendable assets in pursuit of corporate profits.

Yet, amidst the stark realities uncovered in these pages, there is also room for hope and possibility. The very act of questioning capitalism's legitimacy opens the door to envisioning alternatives and pathways towards a more just and equitable society. By exposing the inherent injustices of capitalism and challenging its entrenched systems of power, we take the first steps towards liberation and emancipation from the chains of exploitation.

The conclusion of "Is Capitalism Slavery?" is not one of resignation but of empowerment. It is a call to arms for individuals to join together in solidarity, to challenge the status quo, and to demand systemic change. It is a reminder that the struggle for justice is ongoing and that each of us has a role to play in dismantling systems of oppression and building a more humane and compassionate world.

As the final pages turn, readers are left with a profound sense of urgency and responsibility. The question posed in the title is not merely academic but serves as a rallying cry for action. It is a challenge to confront the injustices of capitalism head-on, to imagine alternative futures, and to work towards a world where exploitation and oppression are relics of the past.

In the end, "Is Capitalism Slavery?" leaves us with a powerful reminder that the fight for freedom and justice is far from over.

Related book by Greg V. Jack

Freedom In Capitalism

Or visit Greg V. Jack author page for more books

www.ingramcontent.com/pod-product-compliance
Lightning Source LLC
Chambersburg PA
CBHW072335270726
48659CB00022B/1608